MIGHTY MACHINES

# Scrapers

by Derek Zobel

BLASTOFF! READERS 1

BELLWETHER MEDIA • MINNEAPOLIS, MN

Note to Librarians, Teachers, and Parents:

**Blastoff! Readers** are carefully developed by literacy experts and combine standards-based content with developmentally appropriate text.

**Level 1** provides the most support through repetition of high-frequency words, light text, predictable sentence patterns, and strong visual support.

**Level 2** offers early readers a bit more challenge through varied simple sentences, increased text load, and less repetition of high-frequency words.

**Level 3** advances early-fluent readers toward fluency through increased text and concept load, less reliance on visuals, longer sentences, and more literary language.

**Level 4** builds reading stamina by providing more text per page, increased use of punctuation, greater variation in sentence patterns, and increasingly challenging vocabulary.

**Level 5** encourages children to move from "learning to read" to "reading to learn" by providing even more text, varied writing styles, and less familiar topics.

Whichever book is right for your reader, Blastoff! Readers are the perfect books to build confidence and encourage a love of reading that will last a lifetime!

This edition first published in 2010 by Bellwether Media, Inc.



Library of Congress Cataloging-in-Publication Data
Zobel, Derek, 1983-
Scrapers / by Derek Zobel.
p. cm. – (Blastoff! readers. Mighty machines)
Includes bibliographical references and index.
Summary: "Simple text and full color photographs introduce beginning readers to scrapers. Developed by literary experts for students in kindergarten through grade 3"–Provided by publisher.
ISBN 978-1-60014-271-0 (hardcover : alk. paper)
1. Scrapers (Earthmoving machinery)–Juvenile literature. I. Title.

TA725.Z628 2010
621.8'65–dc22

2009008279

# Contents

A scraper is an **earth mover**. It is used to scrape the ground.

CAT
627G

A scraper has a front part and a rear part.

front part
CATERPILLAR
rear part

The front part of a scraper has an **engine**.

623G
CAT
623G

The driver sits
in a **cab**.
The cab is in
the front part
of a scraper.

cab

The rear part of a scraper has a **hopper**. The hopper has a blade to cut into the ground.

CAT
CAT
631G
hopper

The cab has a **lever**. The lever moves the hopper up and down.

lever

The hopper on this scraper is full of dirt. The driver closes the **apron**.

apron
CAT
657E
657E
CAT

The driver moves the full scraper over to the **fill area**.

CAT
CATERPILL

The driver
lifts the apron
and pushes
the **ejector**
forward.
The dirt is
pushed out.
Good work!

CAT
ejector

# Glossary

**apron**–the door that opens and closes on a hopper

**cab**–the place where the driver sits

**earth mover**–a big, heavy machine used to move dirt and rock

**ejector**–the back wall of a hopper; it moves forward to push dirt out of the hopper.

**engine**–a machine that makes a vehicle move

**fill area**–the area where a scraper unloads dirt

**hopper**–a bin that holds dirt; the hopper on a scraper picks up dirt and rock.

**lever**–a handle that can move up and down; the lever on a scraper moves the hopper up and down.

# To Learn More

## AT THE LIBRARY

Mezzanotte, Jim. *Giant Scrapers.* Milwaukee, Wisc.: Gareth Stevens, 2005.

Randolph, Joanne. *Road Scrapers.* New York, N.Y.: Rosen, 2002.

## ON THE WEB

Learning more about mighty machines is as easy as 1, 2, 3.

1. Go to www.factsurfer.com.
2. Enter "mighty machines" into the search box.
3. Click the "Surf" button and you will see a list of related Web sites.

With factsurfer.com, finding more information is just a click away.

# Index

The images in this book are reproduced through the courtesy of: Caterpilar Inc., front cover, pp. 5, 9, 13, 15, 17, 19, 21; Daimler Chrysler/Transtock/Alamy, p. 7; Robert Pernell, p. 11.